COMPOSTIIONS FOR BASS

I0812324

BY

TYRONE BROWN

Online Audio www.melbay.com/21118BCDEB

Audio Contents

1 2 3 4 5 6 7 8 9 0

Visit us on the Web at www.melbay.com — E-mail us at email@melbay.com

In memory of my Mother, Father and Brother;
Rebecca, Colbert and Ronald

Also dedicated to my sister, Gloria Patterson
and my first bass and music teacher, John Ellis.

In appreciation of the PEW Fellowships in the Arts Foundation

CONTENTS

Credits:

Audio recorded at Radio Active Productions
Daoud Shaw owner/engineer
8527 Glen Campbell Road – Philadelphia, PA 19128 USA
phone/fax: 215–483–0723 www.radioactiveproductions.com

My Instruments:

Pollmann Acoustic Bass with Obligato Strings by Pirastro
Taylor Acoustic Bass Guitar with Elixir Strings by Gore
Bow by Elizabeth Vander Veer Shaak

I hope you enjoy listening to and playing this music, and please feel free to interpret or arrange any of the pieces as your creativity dictates.

For updates on new CD releases with my string sextet and other artists please check my website periodically at: www.dreamboxmedia.com/tyronebrown.htm

Tyrone Brown – January 2004

TYRONE BROWN
BIOGRAPHICAL HIGHLIGHTS

SELECTED AWARDS AND HONORS
2003 PEW Fellowships in the Arts – Composition
2001 Pennsylvania Council on the Arts Fellowship – Composition
2000 Song of the Sun by the Tyrone Brown String Sextet selected
'CD of the Year' by Dr. Jack Buerkle, Jazz Historian and Radio Host
1994 Outstanding Achievement and Contribution – Council of Jazz Advocates
1994 Best Acoustic Bass – Jazz Philadelphia Magazine Reader's Choice
1993 Best Acoustic Bass – Jazz Philadelphia Magazine Reader's Choice
1983 National Endownment for the Arts Fellowhip – Composition
1978 Gold Recording – Reed Seed, Grover Washington, Jr. & Locksmith
1977 Gold Recording – Live at the Bijou, Grover Washington, Jr. & Locksmith

SELECTED RECORDING HISTORY
2003 Recorded 100 CD's to date including five with Max Roach, four with Pat Martino, five with Odean Pope, three with Bobby Zankel, three with Catalyst, two with Rachelle Ferrell, one with Dave Burrell, one with Cecil Bridgewater, five with Grover Washington, Jr., three with Gay Pearson, and two with the Tyrone Brown String Sextet.

SELECTED PERFORMING COLLABORATIONS
2003 Also Performed to date with: Freddie Hubbard, Etta Jones, Dizzy Gillespie, David Murray, Stanley Turrentine, Lou Rawls, Kenny Barron, Johnny Hartman, Vanessa Rubens, Clark Terry, Sonny Fortune, Phil Woods, Sir Roland Hanna, Nat Adderly, Benny Golson, J. J. Johnson, John Blake, Donald Byrd, Jon Faddis, Steve Marcus, Sam Rivers, Jack Wilkins, Richie Cole, Jackie King, Clark Terry, Mulgrew Miller, Al Grey, Mickey Roker, Billy Paul, Archie Shepp, Sonny Stitt, Eddie Lockjaw Davis, Frank Foster, Red Garland, Harold Mabern, Roy Eldredge, Johnny Coles, Jimmy Heath, Albert Tooty Heath, John Gilmore, Bobby Durham, Kenny Clark, Basso Neauvou – Jamaladeen Tacuma/Gerald Veasley/Warren Oree/Webb Thomas, Philly Joe Jones, Rosella C. Washington, Michael Brecker, Bob Miles, Jimmy Bruno, Hank Mobley, Trudy Pitts & Mr. C, Eric Nemeyer, Byard Lancaster, Sumi Tonooka, Trio Basso – Reggie Workman/Lee Smith, Shirley Scott, Susan Werner, Poets: Sonia Sanchez, Pheralyn Dove, Dancers: Germaine Ingram, La Vaughn Robinson, Harpist: Gloria Galante and Guest artist with the Philadelphia Orchesta.

SELECTED TEACHING EXPERIENCES
2003 Experiences to date include Jamey Aebersold's Jazz Camps at Illinois State University and Brigham Young University. Director, Model Cities Music Dept. Philadelphia, PA. Workshops, Temple University and University of the Arts, Philadelphia, P.A. Master Classes, Jerusalem, Israel and Barcelona, Spain.

BASICALLY KARR

Track #1

By Tyrone Brown

(duet version)

2.
Bridge
G–11
F maj7
E♭ maj7
F–11
F–11
E♭ maj7
E♭ maj7
F–11
G–11
F–11
3.
D. S. al Coda
E♭
G–11
G–11
F
Fine
Solo
(transcribed solo optional)
F maj7
G–11
G–11

F maj7
F maj7
G–11
G–11
F maj7
F maj7
G–11
G–11
F maj7
F maj7
G–11
G–11
F maj7
E♭ maj7
F–11

F–11
E♭ maj7
E♭ maj7
F–11
F–11
E♭ maj7
F maj7
G–11
G–11
F maj7
F maj7
G–11
G–11
F maj7

Intro ♩ = 104
(A Phrygian)
Pizzicato
(No repeat on D.S.)
slide
(play first 3 melody notes 8vb on repeat)
slide
(play first 3 melody notes 8vb on repeat)
slide
(continue slide to A in next bar)

slide
slide
slide

♩ = 144

A tempo
D. S. al Coda
Coda
slide and fade
Fine.

WALKING SONG

Track #3

By Tyrone Brown

Solo (transcribed solo optional) (chord pattern continued)

D. S. al Fine

"Tyrone Brown's playing reminds me of those colorful bouncing balls you see at a carnival."
– Dizzy Gillespie

"In my opinion, Tyrone Brown is one of America's most prolific bassists; remaining totally active with new music."
– Pat Martino

"Tyrone Brown projects a fantastic mood through his compositions and playing. His groove is always present."
– Rufus Reid

NO TIME FOR TEARS

Track #4

By Tyrone Brown

(for acoustic bass guitar)

Fade
D. C. al Coda
Coda
Fade
Fine.

GONE NOW

Track #5

By Tyrone Brown

slide
slide
slide bottom note
sl.

Solo (transcribed solo optional)

D. S. al Coda
Coda
Vamp and fade
(adlib)
Fine.

DEAR MR. ROACH

Track #6

By Tyrone Brown

(duet version)

3
C–7
F7
B♭7
E7
D♭7
G7♭5♯9
Fine
Solo (transcribed solo optional)
B♭7
E7
D♭7
G7
B♭7
E7
(Play double stops 8va)
D♭7
G7
E♭7
A7
G♭7
C7
B♭7
E7
D♭7
G7
D♭–7
G♭7
C–7
F7
B♭7
E7
D♭7
G7

B♭7 E7 D♭7 G7 B♭7 E7
D♭7 G7 E♭7 A7 G♭7 C7
B♭7 E7 D♭7 G7 D♭–7 G♭7
C–7 F7 B♭7 E7 D♭7 G7
B♭7 E7 D♭7 G7 B♭7 E7

D♭7 G7 E♭7 A7 G♭7 C7
B♭7 E7 D♭7 G7 D♭–7 G♭7
C–7 F7 B♭7 E7 D♭7 G7
D. C. al Fine

THEME FROM EMERALD VALLEY

By Tyrone Brown

(for acoustic bass guitar) Track #7

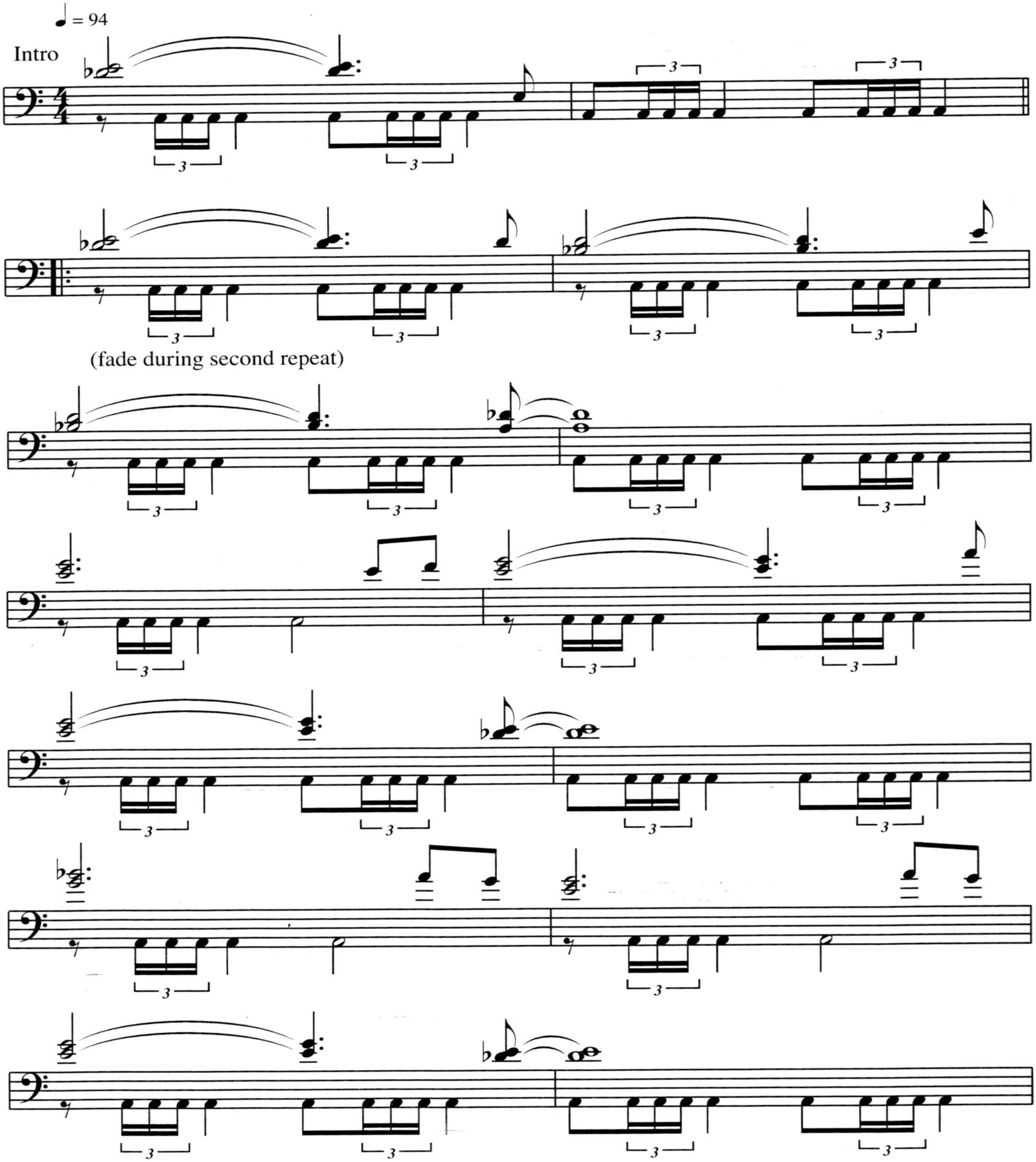

1.
2.

CLOUD FLOWERS

Track #8

By Tyrone Brown

(duet version)

Interlude – Latin Feel
A–7
A♭ maj7♯5
D♭maj7♭5
G7♯5
Amaj7
D♭7/G
Swing
Solo (transcribed solo optional)
(observe pickup on D. S. only)
Cmaj9
D♭maj9
Cmaj9
D♭maj9
arco
(chord pattern continued)

D. S. al Coda
Coda
Cmaj9
D♭maj9
(chord pattern continued)
ritard
Fine.

EL MONTE

Track #9

By Tyrone Brown

"Tyrone Brown is one of the most creative musicians I have ever worked with.
He is a fine composer and a virtuoso instrumentalist."
– Max Roach

"Tyrone Brown has an unaparalleled breath of musical vision, without diluting the music's content, or drifting into 'commercial–crossover' triviality. He also swings his ears off."
– Michael Shahan Associate Principal Bassist Philadelphia Orchestra

"Tyrone Brown sure can groove."
– Kenny Kirkland

HYMN

Track #10

By Tyrone Brown

D. S. al Coda
ritard
Fine.

EXCELLENCE IN MUSIC

MEL BAY®

Since 1947